PENNY SHARMAN
THE DAY BEFORE JOY

Newton-le-Willows

Published in the United Kingdom in 2020
by The Knives Forks And Spoons Press,
51 Pipit Avenue,
Newton-le-Willows,
Merseyside,
WA12 9RG.

ISBN 978-1-912211-75-3

Copyright © Penny Sharman, 2020.

The right of Penny Sharman to be identified as the author of this work has been asserted by them in accordance with the Copyrights, Designs and Patents Act of 1988. All rights reserved. No part of this publication may be reproduced, stored in a retrieval system, transmitted in any form or by any means, electronic, photocopying, recording or otherwise, without prior permission of the publisher.

Notes & Acknowledgements:

'Silverfish' was first published in *Obsessed with Pipework*.

All artwork is by Penny Sharman www.pennysharman.co.uk

I would like to thank Alec Newman for having faith in my work and smiling with me. I couldn't possibly list all the wonderful poets that have entered my worldview of poetry and inspired my work there are so many.

Thanks also to Mark Waldron, George Szirtes, Ailsa Cox and Ilya Kaminsky for taking the time to read this book and to write their gems for me. May the world always hold on to creativity and free expression.

Contents

Alphabet Love	7
Carew	8
Crime Lake	10
Diamonds and Snakes	11
Dragon Lines at Culbone	14
Flawed	15
Free Falling	16
Room with a Hundred Bowls	18
Scene	19
Self Portrait with Goldfinches	21
Self-portraits	22
Semi-detached	23
Serpentine	25
Harbour	26
Riff on Water	28
Ship in a Bottle	30
Silverfish	31
Snow Disappearing from the Allotments	34
St Cuthbert's Cave	35
Tree Bumblebee	37
Views on the White Space	39
Possible Side Effects	41
Adonis Blue	43
Golden Angel	44
I Hold You	47
White Feather	48

Thrift	52
Forgetting	54
A Green Woodpecker's Philosophy	56
Bee Song	59
Bee Song	61
Bear	62
A weeping willow's extinction	63
Aerial	65
Beauty of White	66
'Our greatest blessings come to us by way of madness' – Socrates	68
Cinderella	69
Experiencing Bill Viola	70
Feet	72
Fire Ceremony for the Sun Dog	73
Friendship	76
Headstand	77
Purple Hills	78
Wall with Green Door	80
Ghost Tree	82
Hen Harrier	83
Kintsukuroi	85
Parasite	86
Panic Room	87

I would like to dedicate *The Day Before Joy* to my mum Joan Dorothy Sharman and my dad Peter Leopold Sharman who are always in my heart so many years after their passing; and to let them know even though we had a rocky road something of them remains in these pages and images today.

Penny Sharman

soleil

Alphabet Love

Before you arrived all frogs in my garden were made of clay. **C**ircumference of days and nights heard you singing somewhere else. **D**ecember was always the warmest month with you, lost in white cotton sheets and red wine. **E**ndorphin life entered the front door in the palms of your hand, within slate blue eyes. **F**orget. It's so easy to leave all those lonely years behind. **G**rowing bluebell buds under the Acer reminds us both of happy bees, the golden honey. **H**ellebores, my favorites in spring, a sign like birdsong, return of warmth in the bones. **I** don't know what I'd do without you now that your roots are entwined with mine. **J**uice. I'll remind you of oranges, blackberries, strawberries, a fruit salad of lips kissing, the etcetera. **K**undalini. Even though our aged love is bereft of coitus, we spoon, we spoon, we spoon. **L**emon zest. I know I can suck a slice no problem, can't see you even trying; how I love our differences. **M**an, I love how you get my elfness, my Sagittarian temper, my sensitivity to sound and light. **N**o, no way will I let you run away from this heaven. **O**h please, people who wish for love don't give up. **P**enelope waited for twenty years to see Odysseus once more, I waited sixty-five for you. **Q**uerencia is a place where you feel safe, like I do with you. **R**idiculous that you have kept me waiting, even if your toenails are yellow and hard, I love you. **S**illy me, silly you, thinking we could avoid each other for much longer. *Carpe diem.* **T**antalizingly, we write words in Moomintroll cards, we take care to remember the gift. **U**nder a full moon I explode. **A**m I angel or devil, you ask me, you run for cover. **V**iolet love, tiny face amongst green leaves, pick me a posy in April's yearning. **W**indflower, your dreams of cypher and code, how you nurture my woodland floor. **X**-rated, sometimes words don't manifest fast enough, like I'm sorry I hurt you today. **Y**our skin puzzles me, it's so smooth, Adonis, boy man, lines on your face tell me your age. **Z**oom. Zoom. Can't you stop the second hand turning?

Penny Sharman
Carew

I can't stop the water coming in,
your breath loud behind the castle door.

I can't stop the earth rolling back to water,
the slack slate, red brick, clay and mud,

the gravel biscuits under my feet. The grits
move over and over, guided by the moon.

The moon that whispers to red mullet feeding,
the trippers that stare, the stones still grinding

wheat for flour in the silence and noise at
the tidal mill, where a cabbage white flies low

over the singing river, where I can't stop the
water coming in, your breath behind the door.

The Day Before Joy

arbre d'armour

Penny Sharman

Crime Lake
Circa 1900-2019

It's an old local name for a meadow/patch of land/lea/mead/ground/soil. It's never easy to find the root of this towpath/the memory of boats on water. Now it's full of beggars, the coots/moorhens/mallards/swans/a squadron of Canada geese/bird-shit/wings in flight. It was a mistake/a landslip/a coming together of waters. It's been a water world for rowing boats/steamboat trips/a playground for men in hats/ladies in long dresses and parasols. It's been home to tea rooms/voices and songs/all those happy days. Now it's a beauty spot/an Eden full of ghostly bricks and drowned houses/it's a local word for meadow/pasture/glebe/mead. Now it flaunts a single fisherman and fly tippers/another plastic island in the making/guilt in the badlands where mayhem floats down the spillway into the Medlock/where life moves over the cascade of locks/where the view is still mind blowing at Waterhouses Aqueduct/where the memory of boats and stick people remain.

The Day Before Joy

Diamonds and Snakes

Look   the light catches the spaces in-between
ladders and stepping stones   green lakes surrounded by orange paint
grit the constellation of words   the plough and furrow the
little s's   big b's   the r and m
he is good on curiosity sees each letter as an image
how his hand brings light to the golden meaning
the dark sky   deep blue the ocean
the desert sky   a lady that dances   a shooting star

a dervish from left to right from right to left
a reading in the tiny-tiny white dots   twinkle of stars
we are aloud to touch this   it's loud   so bright

ten steps
five red candles burning
twenty spent
I've no idea what's behind the icons
saints   shields   love on a higher plane
here are the stone seats and money coffers that need us
the multitudes the wooden upright chairs
empty now
they wait for song
wait for hands
wait

I'm gazing down through Perspex   onto plastic new money
a gift   an action   a conscience
copper   silver   gold
copper   silver   gold

Penny Sharman

The Day Before Joy

'stone words'
13

Penny Sharman

Dragon Lines at Culbone

He said, "*Strange things happen, it's a golden line*"

All we saw was summer
green fields oak beech hawthorn foxes hawks bats and rabbits

All we heard was birdsong
first light to darkness

All we tasted were blackberries
handpicked from the old straight tracks

All we imagined were doors opening
after midnight the unpredictable ghost

All we found was the standing stone
lit with sunlight circled by yews

All we inhaled was a breath of fire
felt something powerful in our hearts

Flawed

misshapen forked bumpy carrots
pocked blemished and buckled
scabbed ugly apples
perfect un-perfect strawberries
my left nostril
the inability to breathe
Angela's curses
David's blindness
your OCD on the dinner plate
your lack of timing
your finesse to break hearts
my fire my temper my mouth
my stupid mouth
burnt cakes   creases in the linen
family traits
the incapacity to learn new ways
a brain damaged child
sexual abuse
the killing fields
my stubborn mule head
my need to be me
my lack of timing
my finesse at breaking hearts
your fears
my fears
my lack of libido
your lack of manhood
the essence of human stupidity to let it all go
to be content
with the gift of love

Penny Sharman
Free-falling

It's the middle of October and
the purple Clematis is still in flower.

It's more than halfway into a moving life
that needs to dance, hear the music inside.

Last year I starred in my Mozart living room
as all my cellular memories mused to heaven.

Like Billy I can leave the room, seek the
starlit skies as toes blaze on an Axminster pile,

my lost long brown hair remembers bliss
with a twist of neck or head.

The spin of a dervish, ball, heel, ankle, is my land of
spice and mountain, a captive in snowfields.

I am Isadora in falls of silk, bare feet on hot sands,
free to fall into life's magic.

Each time I place a sapphire needle into the black
plastic groove anticipation is held in an ordinary breath.

My diary of dance is lyrical joy where time is lost,
in the quickening, my own being dazzles me.

My bones are awake.

Penny Sharman

Room with a hundred bowls
After Virtues of Unity by Halima Cassell

each one believes in belonging
hollowed out centres sing out to others
whether they are birthed from

        clay marble wood
        bone concrete bronze
        skin or glass
        their roundness
        holes and rough edges
        their circumferences
        find a place in the room

each vessel believes in transformation
they know about moments
when light moves through them
and because of their solidity
shadows will fall

each one believes in belonging
that when hands come together to

        mould chip
        chisel sand them down
        sculpt them from
        Earth's rude rock
        they become tribal
        carving's of beauty

Scene

It's twilight
stars behind the trees
a man knocks with knuckle bone

his lantern tells of
seed heads
cow parsley
golden leaves
fallen to dirt

this ivy is a creeper
this bat a flyer

news like four bad apples
rot under naked feet   the turn being

amber copper gold
burnt umber
a man knocks with knuckle bone

palm to us   shadows <u>in the centre</u>
stigmata white skin

light is   light is   light is

suggests time space   life   death
portals   veils   thin   thinner   thin

middle eastern worlds with stars and moons
a lantern with golden thread around his wrist

palm to us   shadows <u>in the centre</u>
stigmata white skin

It's starlight **dark** behind the trees

Penny Sharman

Self-portrait with Goldfinches

You are untouchable,
small darts of light in my eyes,
nervous feathers that jump at
the opening of the stable door.

I feed you, let you dine on
black Niger seeds and you
feast on my anticipation of the
6 o'clock   10 o'clock   4 o'clock meal.

If I let myself adjust to your ways,
be more open minded, you could be
my timer, my breath of birdsong,
my rejuvenation medication.

When you flash your red, yellow, green and gold at me,
I forget my knees
forget my ageing neck
forget my loss of a mother and father,

I'm in that moment with you,
on the feeder,
a pendulum
outside of the window.

Penny Sharman

Self-portraits

Selfies in marble, bronze, plaster, white, black crushed face, sitting on my face, some village idiot. A white slab indented sculpted tears, each drop the same size, each a release. Ghosting black heads on white canvas, four, one, twins, one, one, one, two and the one white face, hard to see, nose a close-up, eyeball to back of head, there are no eyes. Each one a bakers dozen walking away. In small letters the room speaks *please do not touch* the black back of heads not at any last supper, let this not be our last supper, if only your eyes could see our old hearts miss a beat. Five bronze heads, face a full reflection of us all, distortions of the past, dimensions squeezed, look at my thin legs, my fat face, it's just a glance, a moment when a figure passes by, a space machine, you and me in the corners of the room at the same time. I'm looking at a self portrait of Vital, is it really you, white scarf, black hat, mouth, brush strokes to indicate substance, all else ethereal, heads afloat in white space, cuboid box, shadowland, eye liners are charcoal. I'm in the corner, I'm large, I'm thin, I'm moving over the smooth surface, bronze that's polished daily with a very soft duster. I'm alone in this vast space of selfies with a concertina ceiling, so much light raining down on me. I'm so much more than I think I am, look at me here in the shining metal. I'm tired, I'm giant, I'm slated, bent in the convex of silver. On every head I can see the sky. Slap slap it on, a snowball fight on the paper. Slap slap it on the winged steel dolphin, angel antennae and one glass trapped snowball, the perfect slush slush. It's all about balance, hanging, weighting, you know a palpable anxiety, will it fall, when will it, grim reaper thing, but oh how the stillness breathes in a real object, the white sled, splat splat, the lift-ground aquatint. After the last day, that being yesterday with wine glasses, mulled everything, with cloves, cinnamon bark, even nutmeg, every face happy, every mouth wet spoke out loud November, stanzas ablaze, images hand crafted, pressed to paper, leaf after leaf sewn into friendship, each piece of cutlery knowing the set, the growth in a persons rings, like tree wood, heartwood, so much more than one twig, one splinter. We are canopy adrift, clouds of happy happy-happy.

Semi-detached

It's like a set in a play
the drama in the house
wooden floors that
conjure a space
that remembers
feet moving
from one room
to another
every plank
has a memory
of trees
the rings
holes and notches
the lost roots
of someone's head
at the top of house
are beds and windows
that let dreams
light the brain
where stars
and comets
are made
where breasts
are bare
where ladders
leave ordinary
life behind
here is the
quiet and motion
of a pot
that bubbles
over a fire
of herbs
and magic

Serpentine

means snaky, curled, patterned, dark green

Serpentine

means lustre, greasy, silky, smooth, polished stone

Serpentine

means heart, love, wealth, attraction,
means gleam, cobbles, stiles, flagstones,
means treasures, means common use

Serpentine

means meandering, meeting you, marble,
means mystic, psychic, meditation, thinking of you,

Serpentine

means sex, kundalini, means protection from
snake bites, poison, venom, it means metamorphism,
heated sea waters, crafted stonework,

Serpentine

means a substance that holds hearts together,
serpentine means lizardite, it means me and you.

Penny Sharman

Harbour

So many steps
           concrete leverage
down from the quayside.
So many chains
           rusted loop by loop
they fall over the edge to mudflats.
So much common seaweed
           lost buckets and spades
that cling to bladderwrack.
Dogs bark like Gods
           yachts wait
their restlessness thrown to wind
every note on metal rigs   chime
           optimism
for any motion at all.
Someone's strimming grass in Solva,
           well isn't someone
always cutting back life somewhere?
Water flows out to sea,
           water comes in at the land
in this hot October sun,
same as last year when we celebrated
           the treasures
in our palms and eyes.
Everything is in motion
           the black backed gulls,
the tourists toing and froing
to Claire's cafe where the barabrith
           and crab
are fresh as the sea holly.
There must be herons and sea otters here,
           but we can't see them today;
quiet is what they need,
quiet is what we need, like first light
           scavengers
or rooks in the oak trees.

Penny Sharman

Riff on Water

the water is above the mullions

                    a sea flowing down main street
there's no stopping a deluge   the baby is happy in the
un-sinkable wooden cradle   maybe the kitten will drown

the fields lie down to floods   every dormouse has gulped it's last breath
every ear of corn flattened   they knew about the coming rain
the empty jug afloat with   nothing to feed the plump pink baby

this scene makes me feel cold
but I've not finished   I can't see an olive leaf
                                     a white dove
a bulrush or a saviour
in this painting this post card

                    that says water
                    the synapses of electricity
between this man and that

she haunts the moon   full under naked trees
her curls are man-made
                    troubled paper ruffs with a feint
suggestion of features   a face

her thin waist tapers into the flounce
of a full length dance
                    an origami tango of daily chores
washing up   typing
reaching a climax

she's stuck in the middle of
                    stale wood
there's no way out   she's in till her last breath
her final moonshine night

                    rainbows   who needs them now

The Day Before Joy

plenty of red   blue   yellow   purple
in the hills when   moonrise hits the edge of time
look how her feet are glued into living
her crown of blood stories
thorns not always evident

                                  furry ape   long eared goat
                                  horns and hooves
                                  hearts and hands
pray for   pray for   one more day
                                  to gaze upon the light
                                  to bathe in the light

to fill the skull
bone on bone
with rainbows

who needs them
who needs a rainbow now

Penny Sharman
Ship in a bottle

She might feel naked as everyone can see her flags and rigging, her tall sails that go nowhere. She might want to hide from a world's arena, want to feel waves crash over every part of her timbered life. A part of her underside and galley loves the shelter of glass; she knows this bottleneck and reef knot will never let her leave the safety of land. These have been her dry days, her nights when stars come out above her crow's nest; lanterns that guide her shipping dreams of winds and tides, the freedom of salt on her bow, on her figurehead. Inside her corked existence she's alone forever, even the voyeurs, the bluebottles and pigeons can only imagine her through her glass.

Silverfish

little dolphin, little glider,
little beside unknown,
little ghost, silent spectre,
little speedster, little mite,
little Stirling whirling Moss,
little now you see me,
little now you don't.
little speck, little feelers,
little iridescent feeder,
little mystery under floors,
little boat inside four walls,
little speck, little thinker,
little wingless scary dragon,
little creepy nightmare shock,
little tiny silver, little tiny spot.

Penny Sharman

doras glas

Penny Sharman

Snow disappearing from the allotments

It's the coldest day of this year so far,
minus four or five on the thermometer.
Snow is ice, ice is ice, is this a puzzle?

The hill behind this house
is made up of small squares,
inside each one is somebody's heart.
They're trapped in a greenhouse
or wooden shed.

When the sun's warmth does its job
the larch tree drops white tears
and all the white stuff begins to slide
down the hill towards me.

Nothing stops the blackbirds.
A continuum of songs
learnt in the yolk.

Today a robin landed on the windowsill,
his redbreast clearly visible; he stared right at me.

Is this a sign?

There are no answers
in the skeleton
of the copper beech
or on the empty washing line.

Years ago a man built a row of skinny houses
at the top of the hill. He never sold any of them.
The wind chimes in the garden ring out joy.
The hellebores are waiting.

St Cuthbert's Cave

Place of shelter
shelter from storms
this overhang   this rock face
larger than we imagined
sandstone sparkle
to brighten heavy hearts
this lost world of seekers
place of quiet hills
foxhole   bunker   grot

                                        we delved into her forest
                                        sweet-sweet pine her needles
                                        her cones and birdsong
                                        in our brains
                                        our heartbeats
                                        slowed down

slowed down
chambers deep within
believer in landscapes
holding hands
wanderers with purpose
dingle under moss
handwriting forever
place of shelter   bunker   grot

we visit
we pilgrim
we crave
a cavern
a hollow
a den
a lair
a safe seclusion

Tree Bumblebee

the day before joy
my life consisted of
a short proboscis
and a round head
my tail is always white
a bom bus hyp norum
common these days
a plague coming
i like human settlements
bird boxes
holes in walls
but mainly trees
i drink grape hyacinth
cherry
bramble
i do not like rapeseed
i can sting if you bother me
on the day of joy
i flew past you
hung upside down
on the acer cup
saw pollen dust fall
to the pebbles
the bright ginger of my thorax
my fluff and hairs trembled
in pleasure
at sucking
such a nectar
you could say
I'm drunk again

Penny Sharman

Views on the White Space

tiny spec
this time you're a black blot
somewhere in the middle of
a snow blindness   that unforgiving whiteness
every corner points outwards devoid of paper folds
I cannot let my eyes drift from the magnet of death
the void like mother's emptiness
her cold pools within her iris
but here I roam engulfed by white paper
that lacks letters
the ABC of love for
lost children
lost friends
this grief of white-outs
tears evident on the flipside of
peace will come it is inevitable
your voice hits the inside of the room
it nags the pen the nib the crux
slow down you say stop you say
but how can I when there is so much white to fill
the centrifuge pulls the eyelids
don't stop I say go on and on with grey matter not black dots
tiny bubbles that strive to pop in air
breath the constancy we crave
up in the morning asleep at night
awake one more time
the gift
slow down you say
I say give me open windows
take off your shoes and socks
bloody feel the grass between your toes
each fucking blade of wet dew
feel them caress your sweaty skin

Penny Sharman

your fungus ridden inbetweeness
then kiss the earth that's what I say
it's not the end
it's the middle
a doorway
a new beginning
this is a universal truth isn't it
well I don't know
I only know I can hear
tubular bells ringing in the back yard
bubbles popping in the glass of Cava
I can hear my pen scratch a living
on this white surface
I can feel the ache between
my thumb and forefinger
yes it hurts
all those asides
where people pretend to love you
white rabbits   I trust you completely
your eyes have a certain liquidity
I know you have suffered   black this centre of a tiny spec

Possible Side Effects

In the clearing of the squalid
hearts set on ...
                                      one in a hundred with a dizzy tiredness
nausea   depression

one in a thousand with
bundles   breathing problems
                a scaly skin rash

      suitcases   hard-left   clash
                        violent jungle-camp

muscle cramp   hair loss   silhouetted hallucinations
constipation

stones   fires   tear gas
cold numb hands and feet
one in ten
one in a million
a slowing of heart rates

possessions with no borders
migrant   shanty   taken down
asylum
possessions
hearts set on...

taken
bundles   belongings full of

no human sense

police
one in a multitude
in the clearing of ...

Penny Sharman

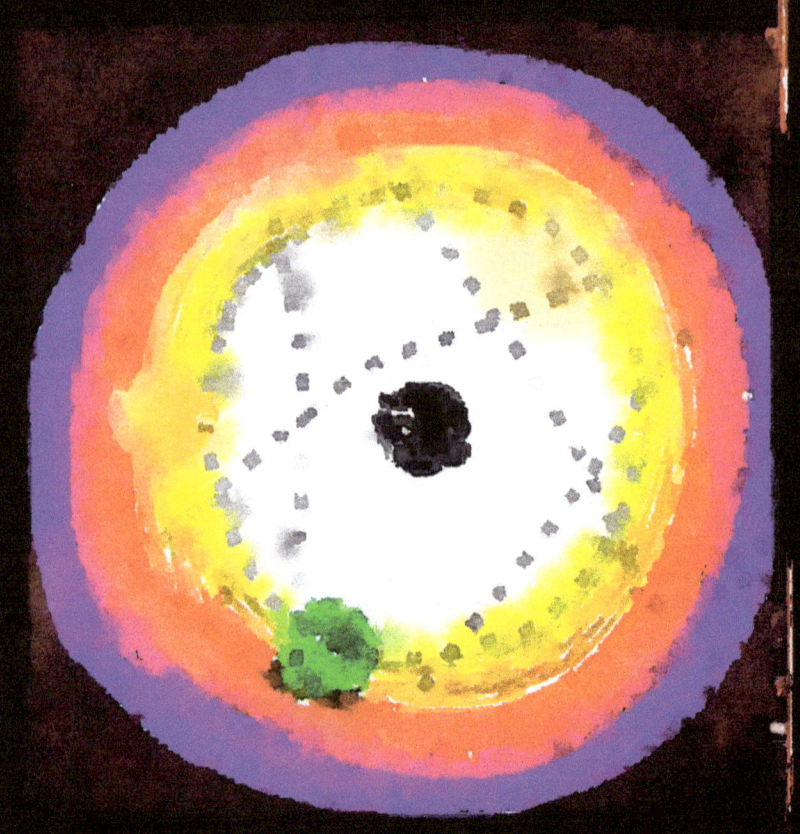

dans la lumiere

I'm so	particular	about	my	diet
	I only	seek		
	the	bright	yellow	sunshine
the	horseshoe	vetch		
		the	vibration	
	feeds	my	solar	plexus

ADONIS BLUE

	my	will	centre	
I follow	the vetch	follow	the chalk	and
	limestone grasslands	the south downs		
	I'm so	particular	about	weather
	I only fly	in	warm	sunshine

ADONIS BLUE

is it love	that	I	seek	
	a	beautiful		boy
	pure of wing			
			sky-blue	turquoise
soft	wings	are	petals	angel's wings
		I am rare		

		is the	hunter	the wild boar
	where			
		every year		
I	come	again	I	come
again	I	come	again	meet me
seek me	in the	shelter	ed	leas

Penny Sharman

Golden Angel

I shouldn't be here
my golden hair   my wings
my beating heart

please tell me I'm just resting
that these lights are yours
and not a spotlight on my nudity

I shouldn't be here
look at my moulded face
serene as any angels'

please tell me I can fly away
far from iron and wood
blaze in your starlight again

I keep looking up as if
something will happen
that my feet will push

hard down on this
springboard
I keep looking up

I shouldn't be here
my golden hair   my songs
my aching heart

The Day Before Joy

fallen
45

Penny Sharman

I hold you

in the white light
when sun hits the washed bricks
i hold you
under this cottage's slate roof and chimney pots
i hold you
steady in your rage
your storm of becoming yourself
your palms wet with sadness
i hold you
behind this cottage's windows
that see life pass by
the children year after year
that happy loud noise
i hold you
close to my heart-song
my will is your will
in this white light
we are our own noise
our songs strong
like a blackbirds chorus
i hold you
inside this cottage's
bricks and mortar
our lilacs and fox gloves
in the garden
i hold you
in this white light

Penny Sharman

comfort

White Feather

i

I've fallen far from your golden wings.
Look at me on the dirt path, alone.
How many fathoms of flutter,
how many hawks have found my smallness.
Look at you, guardian to a body beautiful,
how a sun's storm catches your magnificence.
I've fallen far from the silence of your mouth,
my golden veneer rubbed into this grassy bed
I've found myself in, alone, looking up at you.

ii

I knew before and can't tell you how,
a sensation so light, a puff of air took me over mountains,
a taste of olives, of red berries on my quill.
I knew before I lost flight
that falling was the death of me, a detachment.
Oh my wings, my family of feathers.
I knew the hollowness, loss of sky, of updraft.
I knew before and can't tell you how,
that I would be found again,
that one day a finger and thumb
would treasure the white fluff of me.
I knew my soft bed, my original meaning,
the shape of the singleness of me,
memory of wing on wing.
Here I am, a wingless me,
I can't tell you how.

Penny Sharman
iii

I can be everything to you, a small, delicate, soft, impossible angel.
I can be so white, bloodless. I am shroud to your life.
I can be a message in your pocket, a flutter of someone's heart you forgot.
I can be a sign from above or below, a mystery voice, a relic in your cerebrum.
I can give you hope of continuity, that bread and honey exist in heaven.
I can be sad, remind you of your mother's skin, 5711 eau de cologne, her blossom.
I can be lost, just the one of me, small wing feather plucked by a kestrel.
I can be a lie, pretend that you are never afraid in your yellow state of bird-land
I can be everything to you, a small, delicate, soft, impossible angel.

The Day Before Joy

Penny Sharman
Thrift

Pink, white or purple,
it's the way you all clump together,
hold tight onto sand or grit,
dig into rock, a matter of survival.
I only imagine how it is for you,
life on the edge, wind, rain, storms,
a hotter sun each year.

But when you shine, you blaze,
fill my eyes with your beauty
for miles on this headland.
You are never mean with colour,
your pink palette smudges out green grass,
red rocks, the brown dirt underneath you.

You are never alone or conservative,
you're a Monet mass that looks seaward,
salted water your makeup, abundance
here and there, pink splash of creation.

If only I'd been left alone to feel my bloom,
not molded into another's pocket life,
If only I'd found my thrift like you,
paint myself wide, look out on oceans,
let my heart swim free. Pink, white or purple
look how your smallness becomes a multitude.

The Day Before Joy

memory

53

Penny Sharman
Forgetting

It's hard to recall the nest of a mother,
the muslin cloth and sweet smell of chick-life,
every twig beaked and placed in harmony,
the cup of home. How a suckle's simpering
meant the whole Milky Way of love.

It's easy to hear all my chicks cry, the quiet one,
the squawky one, the moans and smiles, all my
swaddling days gone forever. Fledging is a process
longtime to the grave, it flies from all rookeries.

It hurts to see the fallen flappers who bitter themselves
with lager and ale with puff puff dragon weed,
all their sad stories of chick love, how they want hearts
to soften like runny yolk, wings outstretched for the journey.

It's happiness that brings us together, the grown birds
in their own dreaming days, the cumulonimbus, unreachable starlight,
how our beaks look so alike, how different our dawn and dusk chatter.
Listen, our song birding still fills a human world everyday.

The Day Before Joy

boule d'argent

Penny Sharman

A Green Woodpecker's Philosophy

Every morning at sunrise he calls her.
Green velvet feathers and red punk hair do.
He comes a yaffling for love of her, for her and
green grass, for the leas, his fields of Paradise.

Every spring he hunts for a hideaway hole,
tree trunk haven in a back garden, parkland,
forest, copse. At sunrise he calls her, over and over again
this rain bird sings, woodwall, yuckle, nicker pecker.

He yaff-yaffs his day away and pecks on dead bark.
His green is the colour of a heart's chakra. He laughs away
the days with his long sticky tongue. He dreams of ants,
and more ants, feast of an army.

In the morning, in the evening, the deep throat of you.
That's the way of it green bird isn't it, fluff of feathers, preen of breast,
beak on beak with her, the walk of days, claw on claw;
that rush of energy coming fast up through our ancient earth?

If only I had wings like you, who would stop my sky-longings?
Oh green-green-wickwall-hickwall-attention-grabber, yaff-yaff prophesy,
Morse code of long beaks. Is this what you bark about in the trees,
can you see this madness?

Every morning at sunrise he calls her, calls her
to come to him, to be green together, to share a simple head sway,
to dance on grass at the edge of it all, to eat flies, moths, beetles,
ants, ants, and more ants.

The Day Before Joy

Bee Song

How often I have watched a bee settle on ochre stamens
and fidget itself out of my site, creep inside the heart
of a Snapdragon or Canterbury bell to steal sticky nectar.

If the garden is still enough I can hear a bee hum and hum
at its passion, its craft, its mission for survival. How often
I have watched a bee back peddle its hairy legs covered in pollen.

With precision it reverses into free air with sacks of mead for a Queen.
I have watched a bee scat and dive, find all that's needed for a simple life,
from a wing beat, a soft landing pad, from all the airways of the world.

Penny Sharman

labyrinth

Bee Song

I never felt your last breath.

I waited like a praying mantis
               to catch that precious air,
               to keep it in my heart,
a timeless jewel.

But you tricked me into leaving.

I wanted your hand in mine,
               your happy face with wrinkles,
               but you gave it away
to some other gazer.

When I returned you'd left the room.

 your eyes glazed over
               with black mirrors
               only ghost voices
left in my ears.

Penny Sharman
Bear

Claw me down my backbone
with the smooth edge of your hook.
Leave the sharp point for hunting dark thought.

Let your calcified marble massage pain away.
Leave your fur on the hallstand and be naked
with me now.

Let the gold that gleams around each surface shine
on my skin and inside my heart. Let your edge of
warrior claw reflect metal and bone in our mirrors.

Claw me down my backbone
with the smooth edges of your hook.
Leave the sharp point for hunting dark thought.

A Weeping Willow's Extinction

How will we sit on a riverbank,
come to terms with the lack of shade through a hot English summer
now you are erased from our memories?

Will the shape of your umbrella dome, droop of branch and twig;
all your greening years remember birdlife, the noise of song,
a thrushes throttle?

Here is a breeze that leaves all of us standing under a ghosting of you;
an empty space where only a skeletal you and silence remains.

Will the roots of you forget the mud, water's flow, the flood and gush
when weather is necessarily wild? How will vole and rat, mystery of eel
carry on without your sanctuary?

How will we weep in secret under your canopy of surrender?
How will we hide now you have left us alone?

I remember you, a lifetime beside all my rivers, how my soft underbelly
lay down in your meadows just to hear your song, the simple notes,
your dancing leaves.

Penny Sharman

moi

Aerial

Thin as air, imaginary, this feeling of flight,
heavy in our pockets, the dust of love.

You say it's good to sprinkle it on porridge,
that ideas can be born from just sitting still, no need to fly.

I knew people who tripped out every Saturday, their doors
of perception altered. I watched the shift in their faces
as sunlight drugs hit and Nirvana was present in colour,
movement of a butterfly, sounds from a riff on Jimi's guitar.

Thin as air, imaginary, worlds of flight,
heavy in our pockets, the remains of love.

It's no use escaping to blue sky and clouds,
it's written somewhere in the sand. I remember
the stick you picked up to scribe a heart
large enough to be seen from space.

And those arrows that pinned down my love for you,
so sharp, feathers so soft, they tickled the goo of me.

It's no use trying to hold back the sea,
the honey of a sunset, it's here my love.
At some point soon we will be on our way,
no need for spooning or hands to hold.

We have blazed on solid ground; now we will
be aerial, our dust full of love.

Penny Sharman
Beauty of White

It's hard to capture a snowbound tree with a camera's eye.
It depends on the light, the exposure to snow-dust.
Look how her stillness gives us doldrums after her fall.
Look how calm builds up in her drifts, our compacted view of hard water.
Each time the Chinook wind brings us white halos
over the cedars we are frozen in time and space.
We sit in dugouts and breathe in soft cold slow moments,
the cryogenics of thought.

The Day Before Joy

heilig

Penny Sharman

'Our greatest blessings come to us by way of madness'
– Socrates

The ancients heard voices. **_ghost cat_**   Homeric epics
          people guided   **_balance-fish_**   an internal
voice   **_candle-fly_**   automatically.   a people,
                      exercising
      free will or rational   **_egg-sucker_**   .[1]
a conversation   in heads,   **_hotchi-witchi_**
              distant mental landscape the 'bicameral mind,'
arsefoot   **_mouldwarp_**   all ancient
cultures   not fully conscious.
possessed many gods. Today   **_quickhatch_**   exhibiting
behaviours, forgetting   the term hearing

wink-a-puss   So rooted is our need
                      hearing voices as:
   mildly amusing,   a poet,   confined to a mental institution.
                  'watching television.' The prophets
and gods have departed   and   confused chatter
   must   be exorcized by someone called a 'therapist.'

Dumbledore.

---

[1]. Julian Jaynes, The Origin of Consciousness in the Breakdown of the Bicameral Mind (Boston: Houghton Miffin Co., 1976)

Cinderella

Fire maker   kindle gatherer.
I walk shoeless as the cauldron
boils over red flames.

I'm sick of sweeping floors.
My heart rests by the hearth.
Any day he will   he will.

Skivvy girl by the pumpkin dream,
lips rose ready for the kiss
of kisses.

Black the soot of tiles.
Stories from upstairs
the talk of fairies and devils.

Penny Sharman
Experiencing Bill Viola

one.

In the ghosting tank
there is a white noise
a graining on the screen
a fountain of silver light
a birth
through
water
as she walks
away
to
nothing.

two.

There is no sound in this room a bonfire burns
where sparks   are fireflies.
Who walks on water?
the taper and wick is a quiet monotony
a candlelit patience
an expanding form   through flames.

three.

unidentified landscapes
moving mesh screens
hair curled
noises from nowhere
this time tunnel   human jungle.

four.

Asleep under water
wave motion   air bubbles
from nostrils
rise up   pop on surface tension
dreams with dreams
closed eyes nebulous
out of body   phenomena.

Penny Sharman
Feet

we could just say
hallelujah for
the toes
but it's the heel and ball
the flat solid line of
the underneath of us
the hardened layers of skin
those tiny bones and muscles
that steady our poise
on the earth
they walk us around
allow us to dance the inside of us
to manifest our moxy in shoes
tap, ballet, flat, sneakers, court, stiletto, or
just bare feet
the nakedness of apes
so that we can feel
a sprung floor
the varnished wood
the grass between each little piggy
the sand
each grain
that smooth's away
smooth's away

Fire Ceremony for the Sundog

Tall men and small boys know how to burn the past
with their long handled pitchforks and firelighters.
They have an accumulation of dry weed and mist.
They gather the stories from the valley floor
 and flame the haboob, the rain shadows, grief of war.
Tall men and small boys know how to conjure
smoke signals for a future. They watch the yellow
and orange almanac flare up from the tinder.
They guard the sundog of fortunes, the greening
of our hinterland, healing of the madness of men.

The Day Before Joy

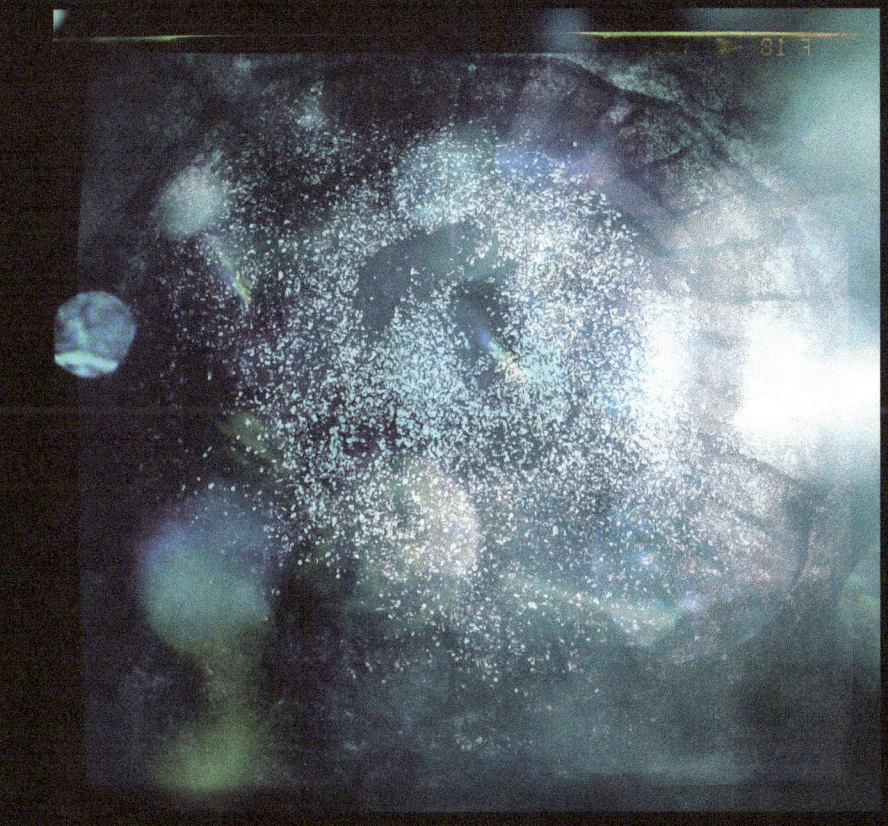

star burst
75

Penny Sharman
Friendship

I don't know what I'd do without you,
each one of you a story behind a veil,
our feelings drawn and woven
into long robes of living,
each olive in our mouths,
each cloud in our shadows
folded with hope and laughter.

Look how we smile together,
hands that were hidden now free,
we each in our own sunlit frame.

Look how we clutch and hold our fears,
split anger in the silver birch.
Together we blow them clear
of the yashmak and yoked breasts.

I don't know what I'd do without you.
How would I know how to scream,
bare my feet to mountains,
how would I know this joy?

Headstand

     come in close
     magnify the bones
     calcium calcifies

     clearly the rainbow dwells in the cavity
     the centre page

     inversion upside roundside
     eyes see something other

when a canvas rotates
whatever the right way up is
pink lines turn to indigo
each grey line passes through
the whole body
the unperceivable   that is green and yellow
turning itself to
marrow
bone
jelly

     shafts of colour light up
     rain downwards
     this image
     white bone
     petals
     entrance to
     black blue

Penny Sharman
Purple Hills

they all look smooth from a distance
up close   on the canvas
paint seeps into the fissures

      rivers run deep
      into the hill sides

      sun going down
      blazes purple

      a veil over
      granite grey rock

a February disease
S A D
is in my hat

but April is in the under-land
in my bones
quills of words

the purple heather buds
that will cover
Buckton hill
across the rift of the Tame valley

      they will lift the ridge line
      all that slack in the shuttle
      we will walk on purple
      depth's in the third eye

'O'Keeffe'

Penny Sharman

Wall with Green Door

Thin blue line
apricot walls
sun kissed adobe
red clay out of doors
flat and smooth
hand placed
desert mud
cracked earth and
one green door
oasis in a burnt out mind
olive branch
where water is parched
inside the green
blue music
red wine
tequila sunrise
chilli chilli
Jimson weed
eight miles high

Penny Sharman
Ghost Tree

Silver fold,
spiritless shocker, replica,
I don't want to hug you.

Silver fold,
sky-reacher, life reflector,
I don't need to hear your hardliners.

Silver groove,
hot metal spokes,
flashy monolith, un-huggable story.

Silver wave,
rootless obstruction, drum roll,
death knoll boom, wow factor.

Silver tree,
crinkle edged robot,
I don't want to hug you.

Hen Harrier

swoop   swoop
beak over claw
sky dancer
just a show off
in mid-air
the rush to the brain
make a pass at ...
somersault   oh the
whore moans
swoop   swoop
hot line hen
court me
court me now

Penny Sharman

tulip love

Kintsukuroi

I'm learning the art of wabi-sabi
searching for beauty in my broken beliefs
beauty in the oldness of me

like all wounded healers we travel
to find the Golden Fleece to repair
the chinks in our hearts

I'm learning how to illuminate
all my hair-line cracks   the negative
thoughts that hold me in the mire

Penny Sharman
Parasite

I hung up the white sticky berries
it was the sixth night of the moon
cut with a golden sickle
our love conjured under
aphrodisiacs
magical plant
mistletoe
needs a
kiss
kiss
needs a
mistletoe
magical plant
aphrodisiacs
our love conjured under
cut with a golden sickle
it was the sixth night of the moon
I hung up the white sticky berries

The Day Before Joy

Panic Room

big bad wolf inside
thump of hard breath
double speed beating
blood that moves
keeps me alive

                                                safety lies under duvets
                                                      denial in the dark
                                                      no one can see me

in my un-facing of
the Cyclops eye   the controller

                                                            i need my pillow
                                                      my sucking thumb
                                                         cover my head
                                                   with a white sheet

big bad wolf
inside the thump
hard breath
broken dreams

d'or
88

www.ingramcontent.com/pod-product-compliance
Lightning Source LLC
Chambersburg PA
CBHW050034090426
42735CB00022B/3481